THE
WEST COUNTRY

FROM THE AIR

THE
WEST COUNTRY
FROM THE AIR

JASON HAWKES

EBURY
PRESS

With love to Lorraine, Don and Nathan
and in fond memory of Audrey May Stevens.

First published in Great Britain in 2001

3 5 7 9 10 8 6 4 2

Ebury Press
Random House, 20 Vauxhall Bridge Road, London SW1V 2SA

Random House Australia (Pty) Limited
20 Alfred Street, Milsons Point, Sydney, New South Wales 2061, Australia

Random House New Zealand Limited
18 Poland Road, Glenfield, Auckland 10, New Zealand

Random House (Pty) Limited
Endulini, 5a Jubilee Road, Parktown 2193, South Africa

The Random House Group Limited Reg. No. 954009

www.randomhouse.co.uk

Papers used by Ebury Press are natural, recyclable products made
from wood grown in sustainable forests.

A CIP catalogue record for this book is available from the British Library

ISBN 0 09 187906 X

Designed by David Fordham
Text by Adele McConnel

Typeset in Trajan and Fournier by MATS, Southend-on-Sea, Essex
Printed and bound in Italy

CONTENTS

Introduction 7

The Coastline 11

The Countryside and Its History 87

Towns, Building and Country Houses........ 113

Patterns of Life 123

Index..128

INTRODUCTION
THE WEST COUNTRY

WHEN WE THINK OF THE WEST COUNTRY, what tends to spring to mind are great beaches, clotted cream, quaint fishing villages, fudge and Stonehenge. As with most clichés, there is an undeniable amount of truth in this description. Cornwall, Devon, Wiltshire, Dorset and Somerset have all capitalised on their attractions as holiday destinations, and with good reason: thousands of holidaymakers visit these counties each year, drawn to attractions ranging from the surf at Newquay to Glastonbury Music Festival, or simply for the climate and location. But to write off the area as nothing more than a collection of picture-perfect sleepy villages is like believing all Scotsmen eat haggis and wear kilts. Geographically it may make up a peninsula, but the sheer diversity of its landscape means that it is hard to group these places together in any other way, and if a drive through the region gives you a hint of the differences, then a flight in a helicopter really hammers home the point.

Few of the thousands of people that come to the West Country each year have a chance to see the area from this view, no matter how often they visit. A trip in a speedboat, yes; a flight in a helicopter, no. Today the uses of aerial photography are extremely wide-ranging, from cartographic and archaeological surveys to teaching aids for geography or history to a tool for planning towns. Less common, however, are aerial photographs taken simply to celebrate the landscape around us, and when they have been taken they have not always been appreciated. When Willi Warstat wrote one of the earliest articles on the subject, 'Die Photographische Rundschau', in 1911, he concluded that future generations might become so familiar with the view of the Earth from above that they could see beauty in aerial photographs (implying, of course, that he could not). He was certainly right in some respects: in the last decades of the 20th century we were inundated with images from above. Not only do satellites orbit the globe zapping us pictures from space, but the explosion of the Internet has meant there are websites where you can type in any postcode you choose and immediately download an aerial view. On the other hand, it is not just this familiarity that explains the growing popularity of the birds-eye view. Rather, it is the medium's

ST PETER'S CATHEDRAL, EXETER AND PLEASURE BOAT, NEAR PAIGNTON

Left The West Country has a high concentration of ecclesiastical centres that span the ages and Exeter Cathedral is an example of somewhere that draws visitors for visual and spiritual fulfilment. It is thought that a monastery existed on this site as long ago as the 7th century, but the cathedral we see today dates from the 12th century.

Above Regardless of the attractions inland, people continue to be attracted to the West Country for its glowing reputation as a quality holiday area. This pleasure boat may cut a solitary figure in the water in this photograph, but the water is thronged with both private and public vessels all year round.

way of turning ordinary, everyday sights on their head, as it were, offering a fresh, sharp perspective that is imperceptible from the ground.

This is where our photographer Jason Hawkes comes in. Leaning out of a helicopter with the door taken off may sound daunting – and quite frankly, from where I have sat in the helicopter, also looks it – but it is all in a day's work for Jason. From advertising campaigns to abstract art, twelve years of flying have meant that he is well accustomed to capturing contrasting views of even the most uniform countryside when need be.

In the West Country, as elsewhere in Britain, the past explains so much of the present that it would be an oversight to ignore its long history. Over the last 5000 years, the Celtic culture, originating in the Iron Age, has probably had the greatest impact on the landscape of this part of England. The Celts established a sophisticated farming economy as well as superior methods of metalworking that favoured iron rather than bronze. Social hierarchy was spearheaded by the Druids, a priesthood comprised of seers, warriors and poets. There is a strong human imprint from this time; defensive works, such as hill forts and brochs, are dotted all over Britain, but (arguably) the greatest of them is Maiden Castle in Dorset. For all their technological and artistic achievements, the Druids stood little chance when the Romans decided to invade and were soon driven into the southwest of England and Wales. Cornwall especially was left virtually untouched by Roman invasion, thanks to the River Tamar, which separates it in part from Devon.

Cornwall's long separation from Devon resulted in the emergence of two very different cultures. The rather exotic sounding names and idiosyncratic pronunciations of many Cornish places have their roots in Celtic tradition, and Cornwall even had its own language. Today, though, the language has completely died out – the last person reported to speak Cornish as a first language was Dolly Penreath, a resident of Mousehole who died in 1777. However, the two counties still remain quite distinctive from one another.

It comes as no surprise to learn that the sea has shaped the land, both literally and metaphorically, and that the area has a strong maritime history. Exeter bears reminders of distinguished Tudor and Stuart seafaring and Dartmouth plays host to a Naval College. But the icing on the cake has to be Plymouth and its historic link to the Mayflower, the Pilgrim Fathers and Sir Francis Drake who lived in Buckland Abbey. Born in 1541 or 1542 in Tavistock, Drake is synonymous with the defeat of the Spanish Armada. In fact, as Mayor of Plymouth he was playing bowls on the Hoe when the Armada was first sighted in 1588.

Not only has the sea shaped the land, but it has also shaped the lives of those that live close to the coast. Before tourism, the sea was a source of work, food and illicit activity. There is an old proverb that says, 'Tis a bad wind that blows no good to Cornwall', referring to the infamous wrecking and smuggling of the area. Plenty of smugglers exploited the sheltered coves and hidden caves of the southern coasts, and although it has been somewhat romanticized, at the time it was a product of economic depression. The Cornish coast is notorious for shipwrecks and people believed it was their right to keep anything they found on the beach. Poor people found themselves within reach of previously unthinkable luxuries. It was only a small step from this to wrecking – luring ships on to dangerous rocks – and a small step again to full-blown smuggling. Illegal, yes, but a necessary source of secondary income for smaller fishing villages such as Polperro. Whatever the rights and wrongs of shipwrecking, it certainly makes for interesting diving off the coast.

Today, the countryside bears deep scars from the once profitable, now mostly abandoned, clay, copper and tin mines. But perhaps the most interesting sites are the many clusters of stones, the most famous being Stonehenge. Dating back to c. 3000 BC, its construction is often attributed to the Druids, although it appears that by the time the Druids came on the scene the stones had already been standing for some 2000 years. Perhaps a primitive sundial, perhaps a place of pagan worship, Stonehenge's enigma continues to inspire people to such an extent that a recent attempt was made to recreate the stones' original journey from Wales. Avebury Stone Circle is nearby, again its purpose unknown, and on Bodmin Moor stand three prehistoric stone circles known as the Hurlers, built around 1500 BC. The name comes from the ancient Cornish game of hurling, similar to present-day hockey. Legend has it that the stones were once humans who dared to play on the Sabbath and were turned to stone for their sin. The two isolated stones to the west were spectators and are now known as the watchers.

With such a long and rich history, it is important to know that there are plans in place for the future. One of the most interesting innovations, completed in 2001, is that of the Eden Project a few miles east of St Austell. This is a global garden, the size of approximately 30 football pitches. The site was originally the Bodelva China Clay Pit, which after being worked for more than a century was coming to the end of its economic life in 1997. The site was chosen for the mild climate and clean air that are prevalent in southwest England and to use dereliction to provide a symbolic challenge for regeneration.

Of his first encounter with Cornwall in the late 1800s, Thomas Hardy wrote: 'The place is pre-eminently the region of dreams and mysteries'. The countryside, with a plethora of monuments whose purpose and origin have been lost to us, not to mention unusual kinks in the landscape, has been a lively breeding ground for more legends and myths than anywhere else in England. And it follows a great tradition of storytelling - the Celts rarely wrote anything down because their religion forbade it, but they were storytellers by nature who enjoyed the telling as much as the plot. This is a countryside alive with stories of pirates, highwaymen, pixies, fairies and giants. These creatures explain everything from the red stain at Chapel Porth (Bolster the Giant's blood) and the creation of the Isles of Scilly (the top of a submerged country called Lyonesse) to 'Daddyhole Plain', a large chasm in a Torquay cliff caused by a landslide attributed to the Devil. And from one extreme to the other, early Christian legends tell how the young Jesus Christ visited the Isle of Avalon, now known as Glastonbury, during a part of his life that has gone unrecorded by the Bible, and Joseph of Aramathea took the Holy Grail to Glastonbury, where he founded the abbey and started the conversion of Britain. Probably the most famous of all stories from the West Country are the legends surrounding King Arthur, who is believed to have lived at Tintagel Castle and threw the magic sword Excalibur into Dozmary Pool near Bodmin Moor.

Naturally this story-telling background has led to a rich literary history. Dorset so profoundly coloured the writings of Thomas Hardy that many a beleaguered English student has been set essays on considering the backdrop as though it were a character of flesh and blood. Daphne du Maurier, a one-time inhabitant of Fowey, immortalised Bodmin Moor's Jamaica Inn for all time, not to mention Frenchman's Creek. Virginia Woolf's *To the Lighthouse* is based on Godrevy lighthouse; Samuel Taylor Coleridge wrote much of his best poetry, including *Kubla Khan*, while living in the Quantocks; and after visiting Coleridge there, Wordsworth moved in a few miles down the road and the two poets collaborated on the *Lyrical Ballads*. And let us not forget *Lorna Doone* by R. D. Blackmore, allegedly based on a true story. It is certainly a most impressive list by any standards.

The sheer diversity of the landscape has also been a catalyst for the dramatically varied literary output of the region. From the harsh splintered cliffs of the north Cornish coast to the gentler sandy beaches of the south; the barren wilderness of Dartmoor to the English Riviera of Torbay; Chesil Beach's bizarre bank of pebbles to one of the ever appearing crop circles; no two places are ever the same.

So if your first thought of the West Country was of nothing more than picturesque seaside resorts, turn the pages to see the bigger picture: a celebration of the landscape from the vantage point of the ancient gods of the Druids.

THE COASTLINE
FROM THE ISLE OF WIGHT TO THE SEVERN BRIDGE

FROM THE NAVAL HISTORY of Plymouth to the stacks of lobster pots at Mevagissey, the culture and character of the West Country is inextricably linked to its relationship with the sea. As you could guess just by looking at its geographical location, water was considered the natural means of transport, communication and industry in the West Country long before the invention of motor cars or railways. Coastal towns such as Padstow were (and still are) fishing ports, with smaller villages such as Port Isaac dedicated to the crab and lobster trade, and Brixham still supplies fish as far away as Bristol. In Cornwall especially, a welcome second income was earned by smuggling and the looting of any ship that came to misfortune around the shores. Regardless of the many landmarks that can be seen from the sea, there were plenty who came to grief on the dreaded hidden reefs of shattered granite, such as The Manacles off The Lizard. Perhaps it is one such ship that is said to appear in Gerrans Bay, just down the coast from Mevagissey, and haunt Porthcurno. Appearing out of an eerie mist, the black square-rigged vessel sails right up upon the beach and continues her journey over dry land until she vanishes into thin air higher up the valley.

If the West Country could be famous for only one thing, it would have to be its popularity as a holiday resort. The beaches here are as beautiful as any in the world, the water quality probably better and while at certain times the water can be dangerous for swimmers due to the rip tide, the huge rollers that pelt the shore at Newquay and Bude make them a mecca for surfers. Torbay, which encompasses Torquay, Paignton and Brixham, is also known as the English Riviera. It gets its nickname in tribute to the 22 miles of coastline that it covers and from the fact that, warmed by the Gulf Stream, it also receives more hours of sunshine than virtually anywhere else in the country. But the coastline is not just about picture-perfect beaches. Character and verve is added by staggeringly high cliffs, unusual rock formations, secret coves and secluded bays. There are surprises such as the unexplained phenomenon of Chesil Beach (pages 27-29), or the tiny Barricane Beach, near Ilfracombe, where the Atlantic currents wash up tropical shells from the Caribbean. While the water can appear gentle and appealing at one bay, it will then attack another with hostile fury. One thing is sure: from the Isle of Wight to the Severn Bridge, no two strips of coastline are exactly the same.

THE ISLE OF WIGHT

For many visitors, Ryde (*left*) is the first place on the Isle of Wight they see as they alight from the ferry from Portsmouth. Its spire rising high over the town, All Saints Church was designed by Sir Gilbert Scott, the Victorian architect responsible for London's Albert Memorial. From Alum Bay a boat ride can be taken to the island's most spectacular feature, the Needles (*above*), which once connected the Isle of Wight to the mainland. Two of these jagged lines of gleaming chalk, towering up to 60 m (200 ft) high, are known as Lord Holmes's Parlour and Kitchen, after a 17th-century governor of the island who once entertained his guests in the 'parlour' and kept his wines cool in the 'kitchen'.

COWES

Left The world-renowned yachting centre at Cowes on the Isle of Wight has not always been so glamorous. It sprang from humble beginnings as a shabby port whose main business was shipbuilding. When the Duke of Gloucester came to stay in 1811, he was frustrated by the lack of entertainment on offer and ended up watching sailing matches between local fishermen. Such royal patronage led to much excitement among the enterprising locals, who founded a club and started to run their own races. The matches grew in popularity to such an extent that they developed into Cowes Week, held in August and now the premier yachting event of the year.

THE RIVER HAMBLE

Right At the heart of the Solent just south of Southampton, and sheltered from the open sea by the Isle of Wight, Hamble, or Hamble-le-Rice to give it its official name, is renowned throughout the world as a yachting centre. It takes its name from the 10-mile long river that flows past the village into Southampton Water, and around 3000 vessels have berths in the estuary. The village fundamentally exists to support yachting, and practically all the industry is boat-related, with the exception of the aircraft-related work at the Hamble Aviation Plant. Cowes Week may be the most celebrated of sailing races, but there has also been a Hamble Week in recent years held at the end of June, with a small carnival, a sailing regatta and plenty of onshore activities.

SOUTHAMPTON HARBOUR

Southampton has had a rich and colourful maritime history and has borne witness to all manner of monumental events, including Henry V setting sail for Agincourt in 1415, the pilgrims leaving for the New World in the *Mayflower* in 1620 and the *Titanic* departing on its fatal voyage in 1912. There has been a port here since Roman times, when they called it Clausentum, and it has been used as a departure point for English armies as well as a landing point for invaders. The port was a prime target for air raids during World War II and suffered greatly as a result, although many ancient buildings are still standing. During the Middle Ages the port was used for the export of wool, but today it is mainly for passengers.

FAWLEY OIL REFINERY

Above Situated on Southampton Water, Fawley Oil Refinery is the largest of its kind in the country and is run by the Esso group. Tankers carrying over 6,600 gallons of fuel leave here daily, supplying up to 15 per cent of all the oil products used in Britain. Most of the output, however, is sent via vast underground pipes, measuring more than 750 miles in total. Fawley pipes its product as far afield as Avonmouth, Birmingham and London, carrying up to 10 million gallons a day.

SOUTHAMPTON DOCKS

Left There are two docks at Southampton, the Eastern at the tip of the peninsula (see pages 14–15) and the Western, shown here, which extends along the River Test. Also known as Southampton Container Terminals (SCT), this dock was built 'to meet the challenge of the ever-increasing volumes on the ever-increasing container ship size'. It is 1350 m (53,000 ft) long – the largest in the world – and is deep enough to accommodate the world's largest container vessels.

BOURNEMOUTH

In the last few years, it seems that Bournemouth, in Dorset, can do no wrong. It has been voted 'Britain's Baywatch' in reference to the belles on the beach and the young lifeguards that patrol up and down the shore, and the greenest and cleanest town in the UK. Even *Harpers and Queen* have forecast that Bournemouth will become 'the next coolest city on the planet'. Not bad for somewhere that 200 years ago was a small isolated village awash with smugglers and very much played second fiddle to the bustling port of Poole. If you fancy exploring Bournemouth for yourself aerially, you can have travel upwards on one of the tethered balloons that rise up to 200 m (650 ft) day and night.

POOLE BAY

Above Poole's huge natural harbour is actually a drowned river valley and, as the most extensive anchorage in Europe, has a history dating back to well before Roman times. Possibly the most exciting archaeological discovery was a 10-m (33-ft) long logboat, hollowed from a giant oak tree and dating back to around 295 BC, found off Brownsea Island. The island is now owned by the National Trust and was the birthplace of the scout movement founded by Baden-Powell.

BEACH HUTS

Right These brightly coloured huts are a throwback to prudish Victorian times, when bathing huts were used as changing rooms that could also be pushed into the sea, thus fully protecting the bathers' modesty. Today they are a convenience for those who regularly spend the day at the beach, and are so highly sought after that to obtain one you often have to put your name down on a waiting list.

LULWORTH

The importance of the coastline around Lulworth Cove in Dorset has been officially recognized and duly awarded various initials, including SSSI (Site of Special Scientific Interest) and AONB (Area of Outstanding Natural Beauty). It has been so highly commended because of the amazing examples of geological folding, generally recognized as the finest in Europe. Lulworth Cove was created by the collapse of a gigantic cave millions of years ago, leaving a smooth, semi-circular shoreline. The extremities of the bay reach towards each other, and the cove is often compared to the south of France. The twisted rock strata are exposed, indicating the violence of the forces which created it, and many geological studies are carried out here. Bizarrely, the coast to the east is dominated by the Royal Armoured Corps firing ranges, which often make it sound as if it is positioned in a war zone, which is why our photographer could get no closer to it. However it is open to walkers most weekends.

ROCK FORMATION

Above The coastline close to Lulworth Cove has been sculpted by the sea continually rubbing at weakened sections of limestone, resulting in the kind of unusual rock formation seen here.

AROUND DURDLE DOOR

Right Just to the west of Lulworth Cove is Stair Hole, a remarkable small cave with natural arches cut into the surrounding limestone. As well as its geological attractions, Lulworth gives its name to a butterfly, the Lulworth Skipper, which was first discovered near the natural arch of Durdle Door in 1832. There have also been reports of ghost sightings around this area – groups of Roman soldiers have been seen marching on nearby Bindon Hill.

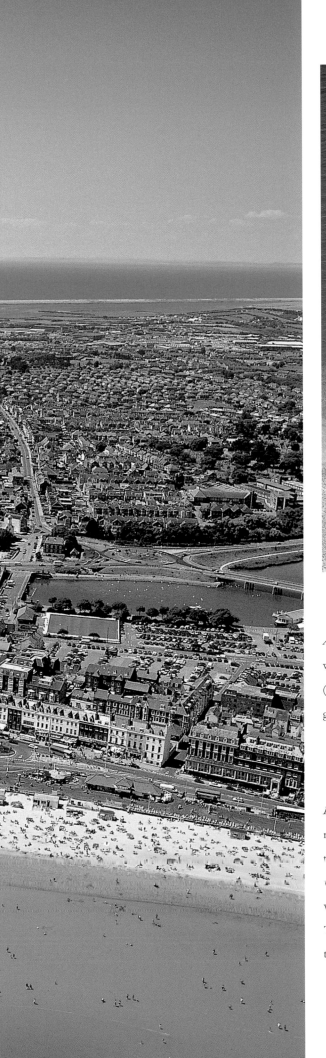

CHESIL BEACH

Above As yet, no one has been able to come up with a satisfactory explanation as to why Chesil Beach, Dorset, is the way it is, and its origin has been the subject of much discussion and conjecture. At around 18 miles long, Chesil (meaning pebbles) Beach has shingle rather than sand: not that unusual until you realize that the size of this gravel is graded from pea-size at the west end, to egg-size on the east.

WEYMOUTH

Left Weymouth citizens erected a statue of George III to mark the 50th year of his reign in 1810, with good reason. On account of his 'nervous disorder', the king was told to bathe in sea water, and consequently made a total of 14 trips to this Dorset resort with his royal entourage. Naturally, where the king led, fashionable society would follow and this quickly brought esteem and money to the seaside resort. Today, the town is a hive of water sports, including sailing and diving, and has played host to the Cutty Sark International Tall Ships Race. The harbour is constantly in motion with fishing boats, paddle steamers and catamarans, which ferry people to the Channel Islands in approximately two to two-and-a-half hours.

CHESIL BEACH

Above It is said that during bad weather – and this area has long been associated with hazardous swimming conditions and shipping disasters as a result of its exposed nature and stormy seas – experienced fishermen coming ashore can ascertain where they are along the coast from the size of the pebbles.

THE FLEET

Right The Fleet is the largest lagoon in Britain. At 8 miles long, it runs behind Chesil Beach and protects many pleasure vessels from the wilder weather nearby. It has a number of rarities in its aquatic plant and animal species.

BEER

The cliffs of the south Devon coast change dramatically in colour. Here at Beer the dazzling white headlands contrast with the lush green pastures beyond. Quarried about a mile inland, Beer Stone is a prized material used in the building of many churches and houses in the county.

LYME REGIS

Left If you feel you recognize the place pictured opposite but cannot remember why, it may be due to the film *The French Lieutenant's Woman*. Based on John Fowles' novel (he is himself a resident of Lyme), its image of a solitary woman standing on the Cobb (the ancient, curved arms of the harbour) has become a cinema classic. Lyme was given its title of Regis by Edward I in 1284 and the harbour was used as a base during his wars against France. Today, many people associate this Dorset town with the discovery of fossils, thanks to an 11 year old girl called Mary Anning. In 1810 she came across some bones sticking out of the cliffs when walking along the shoreline, which proved to be the first ichthyosaur bones to be discovered in England.

SIDMOUTH

With the booming popularity of seaside resorts, Sidmouth in Devon was an obvious candidate to prosper, and prosper it did. With a mile-long pebbly beach, Jacob's Ladder (a cliff-backed shingle and sand strip), a good position at the mouth of the River Sid and stunning red cliffs up to 154 m (500 ft) high, it quickly became popular with the high society that followed King George III. Today, Sidmouth boasts nearly 500 listed buildings, with either special historical or architectural interest and it attracts plenty of visitors who are sightseeing or taking advantage of the water sports.

SANDBANKS AT EXMOUTH

Above Exmouth is east Devon's big family-holiday resort, in no little part thanks to the two-mile stretch of sandy beach, which is unique in a coastline of shingle. It was one of the first resorts to be developed in Devon.

THE RIVER EXE

Left Boat trips up the River Exe are always popular with tourists and during the summer months there is a passenger ferry, which goes across to Starcross.

EXMOUTH

Above Exmouth's early success suffered a setback when Brunel's Great Western Line was routed along the other side of the estuary. It took until 1861 to regain its feet, when a branch finally reached Exmouth. Today, as well as being popular among holiday-makers, this Devon town is home to one of Britain's unique eccentricities: a house called A La Ronde. Sometimes called the most unusual house in Britain, A La Ronde is not round, as you might expect. Instead it comprises 16 sides and 20 rooms set around a 14-m (45-ft) octagon, with a thatched roof. The house was built in 1765 by two sisters, Jane and Mary Parminter, who modelled it on the church of San Vitale in Ravenna, and lived here in feminist seclusion, prohibiting any male presence in the house or grounds.

DAWLISH

The first confirmed evidence of occupation here was in 1044, when King Edward the Confessor granted the manor of Dawlish – running from east Teignmouth to Cofton to the top of Haldon – to Leofric, his chaplain. At that time, like so much of England, Dawlish would have been covered in forest and largely uninhabited. As elsewhere in this part of the country, the Devon town benefited enormously from George III's decision that bathing in sea water held health-giving properties. With one of Britain's safest beaches, the small Victorian town is still a popular destination for holiday-makers. The name Dawlish is thought to have derived from an old word meaning 'Devil's Water', on account of the reddish-coloured water that flows from the hills after heavy rain.

THE RIVER TEIGN

Popular with rowing clubs and for trout fishing, the River Teign defines the eastern boundary of Dartmoor National Park and is one of the largest rivers to gather its waters from the eastern flank of Dartmoor itself. The Teign rises near the granite tor of Sittaford at 500 m (1625 ft) above sea level, and then flows across high moor and into a wide open valley known as Teign Gorge. The lush, wooded slopes of the gorge, combined with the river, provide the flourishing wildlife with a rich habitat. The river reaches the sea at Teignmouth (*left*), from where Dartmoor granite used to be shipped. Its docks are still active, although the town is better known as an amiable resort.

FROM BERRY HEAD TO TORBAY

Sheltered in the lee of Berry Head lie the narrow, steep streets of Brixham and this photograph is taken looking from the town across Torbay. Also known as the English Riviera, this part of Devon is yet another honeypot for tourists. In 1850, Brixham claimed to be the leading fishing port in England, with more than 270 vessels including brigs, schooners and smacks. Nearly 30 years later, the Great Western Railway arrived and gave the fishing community an extra boost. Thus the industry continued to grow into the 20th century, but by 1939 only six boats were left of Brixham's once great fishing fleet. Recently, however, there has been something of a revival of this old trade, and a new fish market and deep water jetty have been built.

DARTMOUTH

For many centuries, Dartmouth was one of England's principal ports with the quay playing host to crusaders, stragglers from the Spanish Armada and the *Mayflower* before she sailed to Plymouth. As Inspector of Customs, Chaucer visited the south Devon town in 1373, and the character of the Shipman in *The Canterbury Tales* is said to have been modelled on the then Mayor of Dartmouth, John Hawley. Hawley was also responsible for building Dartmouth Castle, the most advanced fortification of its type at that time. Strategically positioned to guard the entrance to the Dart Estuary, Dartmouth Castle was one of the first castles to be specifically designed to make effective use of artillery. In times of danger from French pirates, for example, a heavy chain was strung right across the harbour to from Dartmouth Castle to Kingswear Castle on the opposite bank.

Burgh Island

Just off Bigbury-on-Sea, this privately-owned island is most famous for its fine Art Deco hotel. It is actually older than it looks, having originally been built in 1895 by a well-known music hall singer called George Chirgwin and his wife, Rose. After his death, the hotel was sold to a wealthy industrialist, Archibald Nettlefold, who was well-established with the jet-set of the time. Matthew Dawson designed the hotel as it now stands, and over the years it has attracted such names as Agatha Christie, the Duke of Windsor and Noël Coward. Much of the original furniture has been destroyed, but the hotel has been extensively redecorated by its imaginative owners and remains a nostalgic reminder of the 1930s. On the right of the picture is the island's highly distinctive public bus to the mainland: known as the sea tractor, it makes the short crossing to Bigbury-on-Sea at high tide.

RIVER ERME

There is no ferry across the River Erme, but it is possible to wade over it an hour on either side of low tide. It is a favourite place for white water rafting, which becomes progressively harder as you head downstream thanks to the ledges, bouldery falls and the Erme Gorge. Apparently there is sunken treasure around these waters as well. Significant amounts of gold have been found in the drainage sediment of the lower part of the River Erme, and there are shipwrecks too numerous to mention in the surrounding areas. The biggest ship trap of all is Bigbury Bay, where divers have recently found coins thought to be from a wreck of a ship from the Spanish Armada.

PLYMOUTH CITADEL

Above This view is taken facing east across Plymouth and is dominated by the Citadel, which stands on the seafront. This huge fortification was constructed in 1666 by Charles II, supposedly to guard against seaborne invasions. Nonetheless, the Citadel has a number of gun ports facing towards the city, most likely designed to intimidate the populace of the only town in the southwest to be held by the Parliamentarians in the Civil War, when Plymouth resisted a four-year siege by Charles's father's troops. Today, it is still used by the army.

PLYMOUTH

Right The largest city in the southwest of England, with a population of approximately a quarter of a million, Plymouth is the point where Devon meets Cornwall, between Dartmoor and the sea. The city was almost entirely destroyed during World War II, having suffered intensive bombing, but some treasures have been preserved and remain more or less intact. American visitors especially are always captivated by the famous Mayflower Steps, where the Pilgrim Fathers bade farewell to England and set out on their trip to the New World in 1620.

TAMAR BRIDGE

Left On the left-hand side of this picture lies Cornwall and on the right-hand side lies Devon, divided by the River Tamar and connected by two spectacular bridges: a suspension road bridge and a railway bridge. The river provides a boundary between the two counties, and almost totally cuts one off from the other, which is one of the reasons why Cornwall developed such different cultures, traditions and even language to Devon. Until 1859, when Brunel built the railway bridge, the only way to cross the river was via ferry. The road suspension bridge, which runs parallel to the railway, was constructed relatively recently, in 1961.

PLYMOUTH SOUND AND THE DOCKS

Above Situated at the mouth of the River Tamar, Plymouth has had a long and distinguished maritime history. Many formidable seadogs have set off from here, including Drake, Hawkins, Frobisher, Gilbert and Raleigh. Plymouth Sound is a magnificent natural harbour, formed by the junction of the rivers Tamar and Plym. The harbour is always awash with a huge variety of vessels, from small pleasure craft to commercial fishing boats and Royal Navy ships. In the Tamar Estuary nestles the Royal Naval Dockyard, which was opened in 1691 and has been protected since the 1840s by a mile-long breakwater built in the middle of the Sound by John Rennie.

CALSTOCK AND THE RIVER TAMAR

At one of the furthest reaches of the Tamar lies Calstock (*above*), a small town which had something of a reputation for the growing of strawberries, black cherries and gooseberries during Victorian times. This was also once a mining community, with around 40 mines in the area rich with tin and copper. With two shipyards in Calstock, barges and schooners were built locally and used to transport the mined metal down river to Plymouth. The branch railway meanders as much as the river on its short journey up the Tamar valley from Plymouth to Gunnislake.

LOOE

Looe is a quirky coastal resort full of Cornish charm and character and attracts summer tourists by the thousand.
It was once two separate towns, East and West Looe, facing each other across an estuary. They were connected
by a bridge in the 15th century, although the present bridge dates from the 19th, and then officially joined in
1883. During the summer, boats take tourists to St George's Island, which today is a privately owned bird
sanctuary and a paradise for bird watchers.

POLPERRO

For many people, Polperro is the archetypal Cornish village: quaint and picturesque, with a maze of narrow lanes barely wide enough for a car, all leading down to a beautiful harbour. Although Polperro has come to rely heavily on the steady stream of tourists, the harbour is still a working fishing port and is always crammed with an assortment of vessels. Polperro was heavily involved in smuggling in the 18th century, with the majority of the village's inhabitants participating in one way or another, be it shipping, storing or transporting.

THE RIVER FOWEY

Left The tidal water of the River Fowey is navigable for seven miles and offers all kinds of sailing facilities for the enthusiast, including Fowey regatta held each year in mid-August. For the more sedate, there is a passenger ferry which runs across to Polruan; and the natural harbour is also well known for sea trout, salmon, pollack, bass, mullet and flounder, and therefore an ideal place for fishing. The river was once used to transport tin, but now each year it exports around a million tons of clay china mined in the St Austell area.

FOWEY

Above Fowey (pronounced 'Foy') was an important port in the Middle Ages on the trade route between the Continent and Ireland, which crossed Cornwall overland to the Camel Estuary. Then during the Hundred Years War, a group of local mariners recruited to fight the French became known as the 'Fowey Gallants'. They were not averse to attacking any vessel that came too close to the English coast or even raiding the French coast. In 1457, this provoked a fierce retaliation, and the French took their revenge by burning down the whole town. Fowey was also once home to the novelist Daphne du Maurier.

ST MAWES AND CARRICK ROADS

Above South of Truro is the complex estuary basin of Carrick Roads, the region's main centre for yachting. St Mawes is at a southern point of Carrick Roads and is a hillside of villas, homes and lush gardens finished off by a walled seafront. The village has a small castle built during the reign of Henry VIII and based on a clover-leaf design. Its pristine condition is due to its rapid surrender when attacked by Parliamentary forces in 1646.

TRURO

Right Today, Truro is Cornwall's administrative and legal centre, but it really came into its own with the mining boom of the 1800s. Many people made their fortune from the tin and copper found around here, and the Georgian feel to streets such as Lemon Street are a reminder of the elegance and prosperity of days gone by. Truro is also home to the first Anglican cathedral built in England after St Paul's Cathedral in London. The site was previously occupied by an old parish church, and it was only the ingenuity of John Pearson that allowed the cathedral to be built: he cleverly incorporated the church's structure into the outer aisle of the new building. This photograph looks south from Truro towards the coast.

THE HELFORD RIVER AND FALMOUTH BAY

From Falmouth Bay to Frenchman's Creek (immortalized by Daphne du Maurier's novel of the same name), Helford River is characterised by secluded beaches and villages, winding inlets, sub-tropical gardens, lush green foliage and areas of ancient oak forests. Two of the best-loved Cornish gardens are the 26 acres of Trebah, full of giant ferns, magnolias and rhododendrons, and the National Trust garden of Glendurgan, with rare and exotic trees imported by the Fox family. At the head of the river, itself a bass nursery, is Gweek, once a Roman port but now home to the National Seal Sanctuary.

FALMOUTH

Above Falmouth's heyday was during the 17th and 18th centuries, when boats carried mail and other cargo to such far-flung destinations as Spain and the East Indies. Although still an important ship repair centre, Falmouth is largely dependent on tourism.

PENDENNIS CASTLE

Right Overlooking the mile-wide mouth of Carrick Roads, Pendennis Castle was built by Henry VIII as part of a chain of defensive structures designed to protect the shore from any French attacks. Pendennis is twinned with St Mawes on a facing headland. However, while St Mawes surrendered during the Civil War, Pendennis battled against the Parliamentarians for a grim five months.

LIZARD POINT

Left Taking its name from the Celtic *Lys ardh* or 'high point', Lizard Point is as south as you can go on mainland Britain. The lighthouse dates back to the 18th century, but it is not as famous as Godrevy lighthouse (see page 73). However, it was from here that the alarm was raised when the Spanish Armada was first spotted in 1588 entering the western English Channel. The lighthouse is essential because of the hazardous reefs of serpentine rock and granite, which have long acted as a trap to many unsuspecting ships.

ST MICHAEL'S MOUNT

Right A third of a mile off-shore from Marazion, St Michael's Mount may have been called the Isle of Ictis in ancient times. Known to Greek travellers and merchants, it was for many years an important port for the export of Cornish tin and for trade in Irish gold and copper. A Cornish legend claims that some fishermen saw the Archangel Michael on a ledge of rock on the western side of the Mount in the 5th century, and as a result it has been known as St Michael's Mount ever since.

PENZANCE

The unusual name of this area dates back to a holy well, present before even the first chapel was built here: Pen (Headland), Sans (Holy). Whether you have visited Cornwall or not, you cannot have failed to have heard of Penzance, or at least *The Pirates of* – by Gilbert and Sullivan. Once, there *were* pirates here, and the small town made its living from smuggling, fishing and mining. Like so many places, the railway line opened up other possibilities, in this case direct dispatch of locally caught fish all over Britain. Taken from the Cornish term 'Thursday Market', Market Jew Street is Cornwall's only promenade. At the end, there is a statue remembering Humphry Davy, the pioneer of electrochemistry and the inventor of the life-saving miner's safety lamp, and all this from the son of a local woodcarver.

NEWLYN HARBOUR

Newlyn achieved great fame in the 1880s thanks to the artists who came to paint in the open air. Today, it is best known for its fish. If you visit during the day, Newlyn Harbour may appear peaceful and serene, but don't let this mislead you. The hustle and bustle kicks off early and the mornings see the Cornish harbour crammed with trawlers, netters and crabbers as the fish market gets underway, with sales negotiated at an alarming rate. The value of the fishing industry, both past and present, is celebrated every August when Newlyn Fish Festival is held. The quayside is packed with craft markets and entertainment, while in the harbour the fishing boats are decorated and there are impressive displays of fish.

LONGSHIPS LIGHTHOUSE

Left From the vantage point of Land's End, Longships Lighthouse can usually be seen a mile and a half offshore. Its only company is Wolf Rock lighthouse, a further five miles or so into the sea, the Isles of Scilly and then nothing for 3000 miles until you reach the American continent. The original lighthouse was built at Sennen Cove and gradually moved to Longships block by block, where it stands complete with helicopter pad, in lonely isolation. Divers are attracted to the area to explore the remains of the SS *Bluejacket*, which all but demolished the lighthouse when she struck it in 1898, and which today lies in the shallows of Longships' reef.

LAND'S END

Right Anyone who has ever visited Land's End will surely agree that it is a very strange sensation to look down and see the land fall away into the sea. At the far tip of Cornwall, it is the westernmost point in mainland England. On a clear day it is possible to see the Isles of Scilly just 25 miles away, but there are always awe-inspiring sights across the cliff scenery: huge stepping stones of rocks, sheer-sided islets, savagely jagged cliffs and the angry sea raging against them all.

ST IVES

It is said that this Cornish resort takes its name form the 6th-century missionary St Ia, who landed here having sailed from Ireland on an ivy leaf. Once an important fishing village, St Ives went into decline in the 20th century. Luckily, the scenery soon attracted a wealth of artists, with the potter Bernard Leach, the painter Ben Nicholson and the sculptor Barbara Hepworth among them. After she died in a fire on the premises in 1975, Hepworth's living quarters, studio and garden were turned into a gallery dedicated to her life and work. The studio has been left entirely untouched since her death. The works of the St Ives school of artists are celebrated at the Tate Gallery St Ives, a stunning modern building seen above Porthmeor Beach in the photograph on the left.

RED CLIFFS

Above Red is a colour that occurs frequently in this area of Cornwall, from Redruth (in the background) to the Red River and, of course, the Red Cliffs. The colour derives from the tin that is so prevalent around here.

THE LIGHTHOUSE AT GODREVY ISLAND

Left The lighthouse at Godrevy Island is widely believed to be the one referred to in Virginia Woolf's novel *To the Lighthouse*. Near Godrevy Point, which looks across to the lighthouse, is a rocky beach with marvellous surfing conditions, although the safety for swimmers is debatable due to the tin extracts entering the sea from the Red River.

WHEAL COATES

Left At the head of a steep valley, St Agnes was once one of the richest tin and copper producing areas in Cornwall. After 200 years of mining and almost 100 years of tourism, the town retains much of its original character, such as the line of terraced miners' cottages known locally as the 'Stippy-Stappy'. The surrounding area is dotted with pump houses and mine shafts, all abandoned and in various states of disrepair. Wheal Coates (shown in this photograph), in operation for thirty years between 1860 and 1890, is probably the best known of these mine shafts due to its photogenic position on top of high cliffs next to the sea. It is now owned by the National Trust.

THE BEACH AT NEWQUAY

Above With a reputation that precedes them, the stunning beaches at Newquay are a surfer's paradise. The north coast of Cornwall is often thought of as harsher than its southern counterpart, but that does it little damage in terms of popularity. Newquay was originally known as Towan Blistra and was an established fishing port. Then in the 15th century a 'new quay' was built and the town was given its first boost. Further fortunes came when the harbour was expanded for coal import in the 19th century, and a railway was built to take china clay shipments across the peninsula. With the improved transport came a steady stream of visitors, and Newquay has not looked back since.

Fistral Beach and Pentire, Newquay

With arguably the best waves in Britain, Fistral Beach is guaranteed to be packed out each summer with bleached-haired surfers who come to 'catch the waves' and take part in one of any number of national and international competitions to be held here. In fact, Fistral is one of the few beaches that is likely to be busy all year, such is its reputation. Pentire, on the other hand, is more likely to draw divers who want to explore the tragic shipwreck of the square-rigged *Maria Assumpta* that sank in 1995.

THE CAMEL ESTUARY

Above The speedboat in the photograph is more than likely either *Cyclone*, *Sea Fury*
or *Fireball*, which ply their daily trade from nearby Padstow harbour and take
tourists on a hair-raising trip up the Camel Estuary, past Bray Hill and on to
Stepper Point. The estuary is also well used by the Camel Sailing Club.

PADSTOW

Above The church at Padstow is named after and dedicated to Cornwall's most important saint, St Petroc. A Welsh or Irish monk, he landed here in the 6th century and left behind him the legacy of his name 'Petrock's Stow'.

DAYMER BAY AND TREBETHERICK

Right Daymer Bay, a great place for windsurfers and golfers alike, was recently voted one of the top ten beaches in the world. Just outside the village of Trebetherick is the burial place of the poet laureate Sir John Betjeman, in St Enodoc Church. It is said that the church was once buried so deep in the sand during the 19th century that the priest had to enter the church through a skylight to hold a service.

THE COAST AT BOSCASTLE

Below There are two particularly interesting facts about Boscastle. First, it was here that the 19th-century novelist Thomas Hardy met the woman who was later to become his first wife. As a practising architect, he worked on St Juliot's Church and fell in love with the vicar's daughter. Second, Boscastle is home to a fascinating museum on witchcraft. It was believed that Cornish witches could control the wind and rain, so sailors would buy the wind tied into several knots on a handkerchief or rope to undo if need be once at sea.

TINTAGEL CASTLE

Left Legend has it that King Arthur's Camelot, the headquarters of the Knights of the Round Table, was here. Tintagel Head was once connected to the mainland by a natural stone bridge, but a series of rock falls has meant that only a narrow isthmus remains.

SURFERS AT BUDE

Left and below left Bude is another of the big surfing spots on the Cornish coast. The most popular beaches are Summerleaze, with its open-air swimming pool, and Widemouth Bay, which boasts the cleanest, if somewhat dangerous, water in the area. Away from the sea, visitors are also drawn to the week-long jazz festival held in Bude each year.

BUDE

Right Nowadays trade is largely based on the blossoming tourist industry in the area, but Bude once relied on its canal. This was used to carry calcium-rich sea sand to farmers, who used it as fertiliser for the poor quality soil found inland. Built in the 1820s, the canal became renowned for an impressive feat of engineering; inclined planes enabled tub boats to reach a height of 114 m (350 ft) above sea level within the comparatively short distance of six miles of the coast. With the introduction of the railway line the canal became obsolete and closed in 1891. Without regular use or maintenance it quickly deteriorated and today much is overgrown, with the exception of the first two miles, from Bude to Helebridge.

WESTON-SUPER-MARE

Left The settlement of Weston-Super-Mare has been inhabited since prehistoric times, and the wooded headland was once the site of a large Iron Age colony called Worlebury Camp. In the 1st Century AD, ancient Romans invaded and captured the camp, killing hundreds of people. A recent excavation turned up skeletons displaying savage effects of sword damage, confirming these bloody events. Today, the town is a destination for many holiday-makers, and is the second largest town in Somerset with a population of well over 50,000.

THE FIRST SEVERN BRIDGE

Above The Severn River, full of salmon and eels, starts in the mountains of mid Wales and then flattens out as it reaches the sea. The building of the suspension bridges has made Bristol and the Forest of Dean close neighbours, whereas less than 40 years ago they would have appeared very far apart. The first bridge (shown in this photograph) was opened in 1966 to replace the ferry at Aust, which had previously been the only way for traffic to cross the river. A second bridge, built further south on the River Severn, was opened in 1996 and it carries the M4 road.

THE COUNTRYSIDE
AND ITS HISTORY

INLAND, THE WEST COUNTRY is just as varied as its coastline. From the wild, unkempt moors of Bodmin or Exmoor to gentler, sloping green hills and lush countryside, past generations have left a strong human imprint of their existence and way of life on the landscape. From the man-made to the natural, such discoveries often throw up as many mysteries and questions as answers, but where facts are hard to come by, and indeed even when facts are proved beyond a doubt, there are always plenty of myths, stories and legends.

Wiltshire has more than its fair share of reminders of times gone by, with numerous spiritual sites, mounds and monuments dating back to the Stone Age. Most famous of all is Stonehenge (see pages 8 and 89), closely followed by Glastonbury (home of the world famous music festival and a sacred site that has been recognised for millennia and is suspected of being the mythical Isle of Avalon, an otherworldly paradise referred to in the Arthurian legends) and the chalk figure of the White Horse. As much a feature of the landscape as the sheep are the numerous burial mounds or barrows, which would have

been even more numerous had the ploughmen of past generations been more inclined to conservation.

While by no means confined to these areas, ancient tors and other sites are also common on Bodmin Moor. The best known natural rock formation here is Cheesewring. Standing at the top of Stowe's Hill, this inversely tapered granite pillar measures 7.6 m (25 ft) in height. It is thought that the ancient Druids worshipped here, because they believed it possessed supernatural powers. The name was probably coined from cider-making, as apple pulp is known locally as cheese and the circular stones of the cider press bear a resemblance to the piled up boulders. Today it sits on the edge of a disused quarry, which was closed in 1938.

It is not only our ancient ancestors who have left a mark on the countryside. The scars of mining are still plainly visible, especially around the china clay pits near St Austell. Other man-made shapes such as crop circles and tractor lines may not stand the test of time as well as the Avebury Stone Circle, but are today just as striking a part of the scenery.

THE WHITE HORSE

Left Cut into the hill, this chalk figure is a wonderful example of Celtic art dating back some 3000 years. While important historically, the site attracts relatively few visitors in comparison to the likes of Stonehenge. The horse, or dragon as some believe, is over 113 m (370 ft) long and legend has it that this is where St George slayed and buried a dragon. The prehistoric hill fort above the horse is now used as a grazing area for sheep, but from the ground makes the best viewpoint for the chalk figure. However, like the famous Nazca lines in Peru, or indeed the tractor lines on the crops (*above*), much the best way to see the horse is from the air.

AVEBURY STONE CIRCLE

Above Avebury Stone Circle, in Wiltshire, is at the heart of a massive monument complex which must have been like a theme park to West Country people in the Neolithic period. Constructed in 2600–2100 BC, just after Silbury Hill (see page 94), Avebury's two stone circles are enclosed by the vast bank and ditch visible in the photograph, and partly built over by the present village. With the arrival of Christianity, the stones became associated with the Devil, and the Church encouraged locals to topple and bury them, or break them up for building stone. Rescue finally came in the 1930s, when Alexander Keiller, an archaeologist and heir to a marmalade magnate's fortune, bought and restored the entire site.

STONEHENGE

Right Stonehenge's origins and purpose are also a mystery, especially as some of the central stones – rare bluestones from the Preseli Hills of west Wales – come from over 200 miles away, an epic journey for by land or sea for people equipped only with pulleys, wooden rollers and levers. Like the Avebury complex, Stonehenge was created over a huge span of time, between about 3000 BC to 1100BC. Its axis points towards midsummer sunrise and midwinter sunset, which suggest that it was used as a calendar and a focus for ceremonies, possibly by a sun-worshipping culture.

DANEBURY HILLFORT

Above With a history of use spanning more than 2000 years, Danebury Iron Age Hillfort in Hampshire was excavated about 20 years ago. As well as the more usual pottery, tools and coins, human bones were found in pits in the ground that had previously been used for storing grain. This combination of relics would not have happened by chance, and suggests that human remains played a part in a ritual of burying symbolic items in a grain pit when it was closed down.

KNOWLTON CIRCLES

Right Relatively little research had been done into the origin and purpose of the Knowlton Circles (or Rings) in Dorset until Bournemouth University carried out field surveys and excavations. Like other Neolithic sites, Knowlton Circles is a focal point for pagan groups and others with interests in 'Earth Powers'. The church, built between the 12th and 14th centuries, shows how old pagan sites came in for a 'Christianization', and is also evidence of the belief that the purposes of such henges were modified throughout the centuries to suit each generation.

GLASTONBURY TOR

Now the site of an annual music festival, Glastonbury in Somerset has long been thought of as an ecclesiastical centre. It has been a melting pot for a huge range of conflicting ideas, from paganism and Christianity to Arthurian legends and even discussions of the existence of UFOs. The Tor has commanded attention due to its unusually regular shape, which has laid the foundation for any number of myths, legends and stories. It has been identified as the Land of the Dead, the Celtic Otherworld, a Druid's temple, magic mountain, Arthurian hill fort, mystical energy pot, ley line intersection and a landing point for passing UFOs. Excavation of the 160-m (520-ft) hill has unearthed remains of Celtic, Roman and pre-Saxon occupation, but its definitive meaning – if it ever had one – has been lost. Between the town and the Tor is Chalice Well. Joseph of Arimathea is supposed to have buried the Holy Grail, the cup used by Christ at the Last Supper, beneath a spring at the foot of the hill's southern slope, while his staff which he put into the ground is said to have grown into the Glastonbury Thorn.

SILBURY HILL

At 5 acres and standing 40 m (130 ft) high, Silbury Hill near Avebury (see page 88) is the largest man-made prehistoric mound in Europe. As with Glastonbury Tor (see previous page), no archaeological dig has managed to establish its true purpose, although it would appear Silbury Hill was built in three stages starting in around 2800 BC. Silbury must have been one of the most labour-intensive sites in prehistoric Europe: it has been calculated that 18 million man-hours, or 700 men for 10 years, would have been needed to build it. Again, there are all sorts of other stories to explain its creation, including: the Devil was flying around with a heavy load which priests at Avebury managed to make him drop; it was the last burial place of King Sil (whoever he was); or perhaps it was the Devil's hiding place for a large gold statue while he was on his way to Devizes.

OLD SARUM

This huge circular earthwork in Wiltshire covers 56 acres and, although deserted today, was once the site of a Roman fortress called Sorviodunum. Centuries later, a nephew of William the Conqueror called Bishop Osmund built a cathedral here and a small town sprang up. However, due to insufficient water supplies the site was abandoned and the cathedral was moved in 1220 by Bishop Richard Poore, to a site where four river valleys meet. Thus New Sarum, or Salisbury, was founded. The foundations of the original cathedral are clearly visible in Old Sarum.

95

DARTMOOR

From the lush green east, to the starker, less controllable west, Dartmoor is strewn with tors. High Willhays and Yes Tor rise to over 615 m (2000 ft), comparatively feeble when you consider that most geologists agree that this part of south Devon would have at one stage stood at around 4600 m (15,000 ft) above sea level. The moors have suffered millions of years of erosion and the tors are sections of fragmented granite that have stood the test of time (around 60 million years) and exposure to the elements (ice, wind and rain) better than the rest. The tin-rich gravels of the moor attracted settlers in the Bronze Age, who left burial chambers and enigmatic stone rows. A deterioration in the climate around 1000 BC resulted in the eventual abandonment of the higher terrain.

CHEDDAR GORGE

Left Cheddar, Somerset, which 300 years ago gave its name to a cheese, is also known for its gorge. The limestone cliffs of this collapsed cave system reach to around 138 m (450 ft) and were cut by a stream that now runs underground.

NEW FOREST

Below left Strikingly empty, the New Forest is a vast tract of heath and woodland, protected as a royal hunting forest in Norman times. The odd road cuts across, but generally it has kept its almost primeval character. There is now discussion of designating the whole area as a national park.

CAEN HILL LOCKS AT DEVIZES

Right In 1120, Bishop Roger built a castle between Salisbury Plain and the Marlborough Downs, where three boundaries met and soon *Ad divisas*, meaning at the boundaries, gave way to the name of the area. The Wiltshire town has been largely built around one of the masterpieces of John Rennie (1761-1821); the Kennet and Avon Canal. As water in a canal cannot flow up-hill, locks were built to allow barges to travel across the country. Here the water is raised 70 m (230 ft) in 2½ miles by means of 16 of the 29 Caen Hill Locks, which had to be built close together to cope with such a rise. In the early 1800s, the canal stretched an impressive 57 miles from Bath to Newbury and was the main way of transporting goods such as coal.

RAILWAY VIADUCT, NEAR IVYBRIDGE

Left Dramatically set on the edge of Dartmoor National Park in south Devon is a very distinctive railway viaduct, originally built by Brunel to take his Great Western Railway through south Devon and Cornwall. The viaduct that stands today, with eight granite and brick arches, was designed by Sir James Inglis, although the original granite piers still survive adjacent to the newer railway. Crossing the River Erme at the centre of Ivybridge is a medieval, single-arched packhorse bridge, which once upon a time gave the settlement its name.

CHINA CLAY PITS NEAR ST AUSTELL

Right When Dr William Cookworthy discovered large deposits of china clay, also known as kaolin, here in 1755, St Austell enjoyed a massive boom. Essential in the production of porcelain, kaolin was previously only known to be produced in Northern China. Enterprising local families from in and around St Austell expanded this industry, which was conducted with immense public spirit. Today, the clay is still an indispensable part of Cornwall's economy and is mostly exported and used for the manufacture of paper, as well as medicine and paint. The huge white heaps littered around the landscape are waste products of the pits and are known as the Cornish Alps.

THE RIVER CLYST

Just south of Exeter and close to the ancient market town and sea port of Topsham lies the River Clyst. After lazily meandering through the countryside, the small river eventually runs into a wide estuary. The natural curves of the river seem to mirror the man-made ones in the photograph opposite.

Horse gallops

What appears at first glance to be a dry river bed is, in fact, training gallops for horses. Seen from the air, it cuts through the rigid linear forms made by the tractor plough, and makes a beautiful pattern. Much of the surrounding area is made up of the chalk downs, and not far from where this picture was taken lies the huge army shooting range on Salisbury Plain. Bizarre as it may seem, this military area is now very important to wildlife and archaeology. No civilian building or farming goes on there and much of it has escaped the effects of mechanised agriculture.

FARMING AND FIELDS

Although the southwest of England is well known for its contrasting landscapes, Wiltshire and Somerset are arguably the most fertile of the counties. The neatly stitched patchwork of fields and perfect linear rows of crops in these photographs are a far cry from the craggy cliffs that characterize the coastline or the desolate, deserted moors of Bodmin and Exmoor. Whereas the latter are nature at its rawest, these fields show the countryside tidied into shape by human hands.

Grass Cutting

With farming being big business in such a rural part of England, food is needed for the herds. The tractor in this photograph is turning over freshly cut grass. Once dry, it will be picked up by a machine and used later in the year to feed dairy cows. The grass is cut early in the season when it is at its most nutritious before any seed heads are produced. It will then be stored under huge tarpaulin sheets to keep up the water content before being used as feed.

COMBINE HARVESTING

The enormous expense of the modern combine harvester (some cost over £100,000) means that farmers must have enough acreage to make buying one cost-effective. If not, they can commission one of the new breed of gangs that move around from farm to farm during the summer months, working late into the night with their own equipment.

FIELDS

These fantastic fields are a classic example of aerial photography finding something new and interesting in the ordinary and mundane – the whorl-like patterns of ploughing (*above*) and the sky-blue expanse of a vast field of flax (*right*). People often imagine the English countryside to be contained by a wealth of chunky hedges, but this just isn't the case any more. In the mid-1900s, a quarter of all hedgerows were removed, ravaged at a rate of 4500 miles a year. Hedgerows are still removed today to improve the productivity of farming, although there is now a degree of legal protection and the net decline has been halted.

CROP CIRCLE NEAR EAST KENNET

Above This amazingly structured crop circle was discovered in a wheat field near East Kennet, near Avebury, in July 2000. For a long time, these circles have been argued over. Are they a bizarre natural phenomenon, are they created by extraterrestrials or are they merely land art? It is quite clear that this one was man-made, much to the chagrin of those with an interest in what would appear to be naturally occurring circles, and it was damned as having negative and mechanical qualities. This circle had a diameter of 55 m (180 ft) and the central square, comprising many smaller squares, measured 42 m (139 ft) long.

CROP CIRCLES AT MORGAN'S HILL, WILTSHIRE

Right Often complex formations, crop circles, such as the two shown in the photograph here, are usually found in wheat or barley fields. Over the years they have been attributed to everything from hoaxes and plasma vortexes to supernatural or extraterrestrial attempts at communication. Perhaps there is a natural explanation, as crop circles often appear on ley lines or occur over underground water supplies, although many are quite obviously man-made. There are many reports of physical side effects such as nausea or giddiness in people who have visited crop circles, as well as electronic equipment failing.

TOWNS, BUILDINGS
AND COUNTRY HOUSES

WITH ITS GREAT BEACHES and mild climate, the West Country has long been a great resort for holiday-makers. So much attention is given to the coastal areas that, apart from the mystical sites, we tend to forget the inland areas. This is a predominantly rural setting with a rich variety of scenery, but there are also thriving towns and buildings that are just as steeped in history as anywhere along the coast. Building styles in the West Country are strongly regional. In Cornwall, a county with comparatively few grand architectural gestures, you find many grey stone walls beneath slates quarried at Delabole near Tintagel; the most rewarding Cornish churches have the virtue of rustic simplicity. Up to the mid nineteenth century cob and thatch was the preferred domestic style in Devon, and much has survived: rounded corners of cob (mud and chopped straw) beneath a straw roof – a building practice not that far removed from the mud-hut structures of warmer climes. The honey-coloured Ham stone, extracted from quarries at Stoke Sub Hamdon near Yeovil, has graced cottage walls and church towers in many Somerset villages and towns.

There are many West Country sites dating back to medieval times. For example, in Launceston there are the two pointed arches remaining from the South Gate from the old wall, much of the ramparts of the 13th-century castle and a few relics of the Augustinian priory (1136). In Okehampton is the largest medieval castle in Devon, which now stands in ruins on top of a wooded hill, and has done since Henry VIII ordered it to be dismantled after its owner was accused of treason.

As towns go, Glastonbury must be the one of the most famous in the region. As an ecclesiastical centre it is home to an historic abbey ruin. Perhaps founded by Joseph of Arimathea in 60 AD, or perhaps by King Ine in 700 AD, it has been excavated, destroyed by fires, thought to be the burial place of Arthur and Guinevere, not to mention Saxon kings, abandoned and restored. But abbeys don't have to be ancient to have wonderful stories attached to them. Ten miles inland from Plymouth stands Buckfast Abbey, which dominates the small town of Buckfastleigh. A Benedictine monastery built in the Norman and Gothic styles between 1907 and 1938, the abbey took 30 years to complete as it was built by just six monks, only one of whom had any knowledge of construction.

GLASTONBURY AND ROMSEY

Left Glastonbury Abbey was in its day the richest Benedictine house in England. At dissolution in 1539 the last abbot was hanged and quartered on Glastonbury Tor.

Above Romsey is often used as a base for visiting nearby attractions, such as Broadlands Estate (see page 120), but people also come here to see Romsey Abbey, so beautiful it was once described as music in stone. With the River Test running through it, Romsey's roots are as a Hampshire mill town. Grain merchants, tanners, fullers, parchment makers and brewers were all drawn here by the quality of the water.

WELLS AND WELLS CATHEDRAL

Above Named after a line of springs at the base of the Mendips in Somerset, Wells may be the smallest city in England with a population of fewer than 10,000, but it has one of the most amazing cathedrals. Taking over 300 years to complete, it incorporates three main styles, Early English, Decorated and Perpendicular. Outwardly, the 13th-century west front is the most intricately detailed, with more than 100 sculptures of saints, angels and prophets. When it was first built, the statues probably numbered closer to 400, but the cathedral sustained damage and defacing during the Civil War. Inside is one of the world's oldest working timepieces, an astronomical clock from the 14th century, which shows the minutes, hours and phases of the moon.

SHAFTESBURY

Right More than 230 m (750 ft) above sea level, the sheer height of this Dorset town has been the principal determining factor in its history. The Saxons were the first to found a hilltop town here, chosen because of its prime defence position. King Alfred chose to settle here in 888 after his victory over the Vikings. So confident was he about his geographical surroundings that he built an abbey for his daughter, which led to major prosperity for the town. Just over 100 years later, the body of King Edward, who had been murdered by his stepmother, was buried here and the abbey became a centre of pilgrimage. Today, the few remains of the abbey are in the town museum.

SALISBURY CATHEDRAL

Salisbury Cathedral has gained worldwide recognition, thanks in part to being the only English medieval cathedral designed and executed almost entirely in a single style. It was started in 1220 and completed in 1258, except for the spire, the tallest in England at 124 m (404 ft), which was added a generation later. The official cathedral website says it was built to reflect the glory of God in stone and glass, and that is probably the best way to describe this beautiful masterpiece, which also houses one of only four original copies of Magna Carta. Many artists, including John Constable, have found inspiration in the building.

EXETER

Left Exeter's history started 2000 years ago when it was inhabited by the Celtic tribe of the Dumnonii. They named the river Eisca, meaning 'a river abounding in fish'. Two hundred years later the Romans turned up, building a massive defensive wall, sections of which can still be seen. A Roman bath house was unearthed in the cathedral close in 1971. In the Dark Ages, the city was a major ecclesiastical centre and over the years this has led to the beautiful and highly decorated St Peter's Cathedral, a small Norman priory and the Church of St Mary Steps.

TAUNTON

Above Lying between the Quantock and Blackdown hills is the Somerset county town of Taunton. First founded in the 8th century by the Saxon King Ine, Taunton was made wealthy by wool-making, but when the wool industry declined, the town prospered from lace and silk weaving. Profits were put towards the construction of the town's two churches, St James and St Mary's, which stand near the county cricket ground. Taunton is also well known for its production of scrumpy, a rough and ready version of cider made from apples and any other bits that fell in. Stories abound that the powerful alcoholic effect of scrumpy was due to the addition of everything from the revolting (dead rats) to the truly bizarre (bird's nests). Really, it is just down to the apples.

WILTON HOUSE

Left 'Nothing can be more comfortable than this house. It is magnificent when we have company, and when alone it seems to be only a cottage in a beautiful garden.' – Lady Palmerston.

With an art collection that includes 'Rembrandt's Mother', Wilton House in Wiltshire is acknowledged as being one of the 'Treasure Houses of England'. The stunning Double Cube Room, with its fabulous paintings by Van Dyck, has been used as a set for films such as *The Madness of King George*, *Sense and Sensibility* and *Mrs Brown*.

BROADLANDS ESTATE AT ROMSEY

Left Set beside the River Test in Hampshire, Broadlands shares its landscape gardener with Longleat House, the celebrated Lancelot 'Capability' Brown, who was well known not only for his genius as a landscaper but also for his complete disregard for cost. Broadlands also has something in common with Wilton House: they both house impressive art collections.

LONGLEAT HOUSE

Above Standing on the site of a medieval priory, Longleat House, Wiltshire, has been in the Thynne family for several centuries. Sir John Thynne bought the priory during the dissolution of the religious houses and lived there until it burned down in 1567. He spent 12 years constructing the house in the then popular Italian style, and each subsequent occupier has left his or her own architectural mark. Many grand houses were destroyed during the Civil War because their owners were suspected of supporting the Royalist cause, but the Thynne family remained neutral and so the house was spared. The beautiful gardens owe their conception to the 18th-century landscape gardener, Capability Brown. The present Marquess of Bath's father converted the inner section of the estate to a wildlife park in 1966, and the lions of Longleat soon became very famous.

PATTERNS OF LIFE

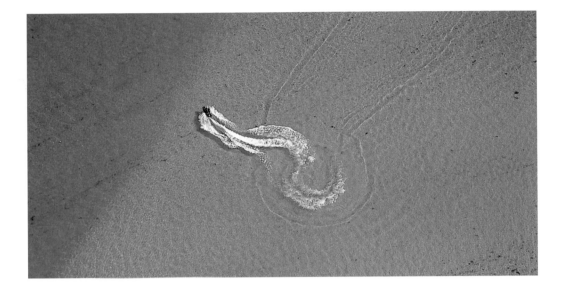

'TEN GENERATIONS FAILED to alter the turn of a single phrase. In these Wessex nooks the busy outsider's ancient times are only old; his old times are still new; his present is futurity.' *From Far from the Madding Crowd* by Thomas Hardy (1840-1928).

From the famous legends of Arthur to cautionary tales about smugglers, the West Country has inherited a long tradition of storytelling, and there are plenty of both man-made and natural monuments dotted around the landscapes that date way back. There is no doubt that the character and culture of the West Country has been shaped by its past and while this adds to its charm, you would be very mistaken to assume it is stuck there. Even its popularity as a holiday resort is impacting on the landscape, with caravan and camping parks popping up everywhere.

The sheer number of tourists that the West Country attracts makes it easy to forget that there are people who live here regardless of seasonality, people who are working to take the area into the 21st century without losing the spark that makes this region what it is. Cornish people in particular have always had a healthy respect for their environment, and have used the elements around them to great advantage. Where better therefore to set up a giant project that will not only provide a place for scientific discovery, but will also educate people about the natural world they live in? The Eden Project, near St Austell, does just that with its mission statement being, 'To promote the understanding and responsible management of the vital relationship between plants, people and resources, leading towards a sustainable future for all.' It is certainly a great legacy to leave to future generations.

From the air, individual people are turned into a blur of colour, smaller even than ants, and all that can be clearly seen are their collective achievements. Such God-like views make it easy to imagine the cycle of birth, death and rebirth that make up the pattern of life. Turn the following pages and see for yourself.

THE EDEN PROJECT

Left Although, like the Jet skier above, many people come to the West Country to enjoy all the activities the water has to offer, there is now a different reason for visiting. The covered biodomes of the wonderfully named Eden Project were designed for practicality as well as appearance – they need to be able to compete with commercial greenhouses. Within this structure lies a melting point of art and science, cultures and ideas, or in their words 'a living theatre of plants and people'. Opened in 2001, the Eden Project's main objective is to educate people to understand their relationship with the nature around them.

ACCOMMODATION

There is, of course, a huge amount of accommodation in the West Country, to cater for tourists and residents alike. From the air, these houses near Plymouth and the caravans at a park in Burnham-on-Sea take on a starkly regimented pattern that must surely belie the vastly different families that live within their walls. Like the tightly geometric patterns made by the farmers on pages 108-109, it is strikingly easy to see the difference between the man-made and the natural from this angle.

124

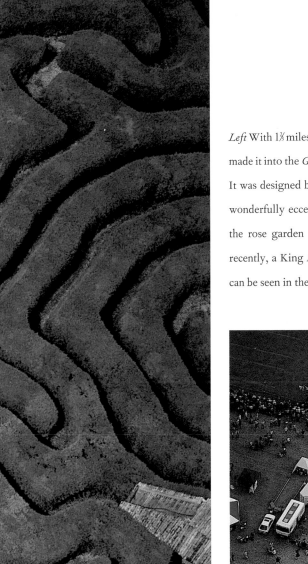

LONGLEAT MAZE

Left With 1⅞ miles of paths and 16,180 yew trees, the hedge maze at Longleat House made it into the *Guinness Book of Records* in 1987 for being the longest in the world. It was designed by Greg Bright and opened to the public in 1978. Since then the wonderfully eccentric Marquess of Bath has commissioned a further four mazes, the rose garden 'Labyrinth of Love', a 'sun maze', a 'moon maze' and, most recently, a King Arthur's adventure in the form of a mirror maze. The first three can be seen in the photograph on page 121.

A COUNTRY FAIR NEAR FORDINGBRIDGE

Above Full of local stalls selling home-baked produce and second-hand books, and with children and adults competing for prizes, this country fair in Hampshire shows what must be one of the most quintessentially English pastimes.

INDEX

Page numbers in *italic* refer to the photographs

Arthur, King, 9, 81, 87, 92, 113, 123, 127
Avebury Stone Circle, 8, 87, *88*

Barricane Beach, 11
Berry Head, *40*
Bodmin Moor, 8, 9, 87
Boscastle, *81*
Bournemouth, *18–19*
Bright, Greg, *126–7*
Brixham, 11, *40*
Broadlands, Hampshire, *120*
Brown, Lancelot 'Capability', *120*
Brunel, Isambard Kingdom, 35, 49, 100
Buckfast Abbey, 113
Bude, 11, *82–3*
Burgh Island, *42–3*
Burnham-on-Sea, *124–5*

Caen Hill Locks, *99*
Calstock, *50*
Camel Estuary, *78*
caravans, *124–5*
Carrick Roads, *58*
cathedrals, *6*, *59*, *114*, *116–17*
Celts, 8, 9, 92
Chapel Porth, 9
Cheddar Gorge, *98*
Cheesewring, 87
Chesil Beach, 9, 11, *27–9*
china clay mines, *101*
Clyst, River, *102*
Coleridge, Samuel Taylor, 9
combine harvesters, *107*
Cowes, 12
crop circles, *110–11*

'Daddyhole Plain', 9
Danebury Hillfort, *90*
Dartmoor, *96–7*
Dartmouth, 8, *41*
Dawlish, *36–7*
Daymer Bay, *79*
Devizes, *99*
Drake, Sir Francis, 8
Druids, 8, 87, 88, 92
du Maurier, Daphne, 9, 57, 60
Durdle Door, *25*
earthworks, 8, 87, *90–1*, *94–5*
East Kennet, *110*
Eden Project, 9, *122*, 123
Erme, River, *44*
Exe, River, *34*
Exeter, *6*, 8, *118*
Exmouth, *34–5*, 87

Falmouth, *60–1*
farming, *104–11*
Fawley Oil Refinery, *17*
Fistral Beach, *76*
The Fleet, *29*
Fordingbridge, *127*
Fowey, *56–7*

George III, King of England, 27, 32, 36
Gerrans Bay, 11
Glastonbury, 7, 9, 87, *92–3*, 113, *113*
Godrevy Island, 9, *72–3*

Hamble, River, *13*
Hardy, Thomas, 9, 81, 123
Helford River, *60*
Henry VIII, King of England, 58, 61, 113
horse gallops, *103*
Hurlers, 8

Ilfracombe, 11
Isles of Scilly, 9
Isle of Wight, *10–12*
Ivybridge, *100*

Jesus Christ, 9, 92
Joseph of Arimathea, 9, 92, 113

Kennet and Avon canal, *99*
Knowlton Circles, *91*

La Ronde, Exmouth, 35
Land's End, *69*
Launceston, 113
lighthouses, *11*, *68*, *72–3*
Lizard Point, 11, *62*
Longleat, Wiltshire, *121*, *126–7*
Longships Lighthouse, *68*
Looe, *52–3*
Lulworth, *22–4*
Lyme Regis, *30–1*

Maiden Castle, 8
Mevagissey, 11
Morgan's Hill, *111*

National Trust, 20, 60, 75
The Needles, *11*
New Forest, *98*
Newlyn, *66–7*
Newquay, 7, 11, *75*, *77*

Okehampton, 113
Old Sarum, *95*

Padstow, 11, *79*
Paignton, *7*, 11

Pendennis Castle, *61*
Pentire, *77*
Penzance, *64–5*
Plymouth, 8, 11, *46–7*, *49*, *124*
Polperro, 8, *54–5*
Poole Bay, *20–1*
Port Curnow, 11
Port Isaac, 11

Quantocks, 9

Red Cliffs, *73*
Romans, 8, 14, 24, 31
Romsey, *113*
Ryde, *10*

St Agnes, *74–5*
St Austell, 87, *101*, 123
St Ives, *70–1*
St Mawes, *58*
St Michael's Mount, *63*
St Peter's Cathedral, Exeter, *6*
Salisbury, *116–17*
Salisbury plain, *103*
Seaton, *31*
Severn Bridge, *85*
Shaftesbury, *114–15*
Sidmouth, *32–3*
Silbury Hill, *94*
Southampton, *14–17*
Stair Hole, *25*
stone circles, 8, *88–9*
Stonehenge, 7, 8, 87, *89*

Tamar, River, 8, *48–51*
Taunton, *119*
Teignmouth, *39*
Teign, River, *38–9*
tin mines, *74–5*
Tintagel Castle, 9, *80*
Torbay, 9, *40*
Torquay, 9, 11
Trebetherick, *79*
Truro, *58–9*

Uffington White Horse, *86*, 87

Warstat, Willi, 7
Wells, *114*
Weston-super-Mare, *84–5*
Weymouth, *26–7*
Wheal Coates, *74–5*
Wilton House, Wiltshire, *120*
Woolf, Virginia, 9, *73*
Wordsworth, William, 9